103 THINGS TO DO,
Outside of Screaming Profanity, Self-Mutilation and Bodily Harm to Others,
WHILE DOWNLOADING

Deborah Ellington

Copyright © 2014 Deborah Ellington
All rights reserved.

ISBN: 0984019847
ISBN 13: 9780984019847
Library of Congress Control Number: 2014913147
CreateSpace Independent Publishing Platform
North Charleston, South Carolina

DEDICATION

To my son, Eric, who always indulges me with my brilliant, and very often not so brilliant, ideas. He listens with a smile and then politely readjusts my thinking when he can. At the very least he is an agreeable captive audience, and at his gracious best, he encourages and facilitates my mental flights of fantasy. I couldn't have attempted this publication without his encouragement.

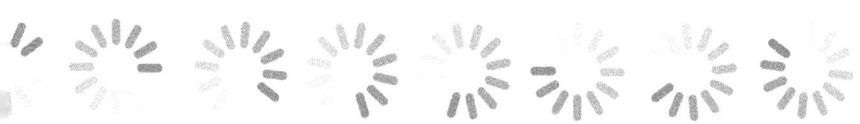

INTRODUCTION

Downloading is painful! I'll admit it, and confess that I do a lot of complaining about it to anyone within earshot, with the exception of the IT department. Without further explanation, never, ever cross your IT department and limit your questions if you value working technology. Downloading rates up there with a wait at the DMV in a major city, being in line at the most popular deli in town, or waiting and then having to watch your cable guy make repairs. In my dreams I'd like to think it could be made fun, but endurable is the best shot.

It occurred to me one day, never one to be fast on the draw, to stop fighting the process and find meaningful activities to fill the mandatory wait.

What follows are suggestions for things to do, some of which I do on a regular basis to occupy the time. Not everything made it into print (note the title) or passed my informal survey (thank you, Sis). There are many options to consider. As the chapter title indicates, this publication offers practical and healthy ideas while others are whimsical, even a few that border on a bit odd. It is my hope you enjoy the read and employ a few to help you occupy your download wait time.

DOWNLOAD

\'dau̇n-ˌlōd\

Noun: an act of moving or copying a file, program, etc., from a computer to computer or device

Verb - downloading

See related terms – maddening, frustrating, crazy-making, annoying, trying, grating, exasperating, vexatious, burdensome, upsetting, tiresome

Table of Contents

DEDICATION . . . . **iii**

INTRODUCTION . . . . **v**

CHAPTER 1 . . . . **1**
ALL THINGS PRACTICAL AND USEFUL

CHAPTER 2 . . . . **29**
HEALTHY AND MEANINGFUL

CHAPTER 3 . . . . **73**
WHATEVER AND FOR WHAT IT IS WORTH

IN CONCLUSION **121**

CHAPTER 1
ALL THINGS PRACTICAL AND USEFUL

1. RESEARCH A SUBJECT.

Take this downloading moment to research an idea, a problem, or a nagging question that pops into your head momentarily and/or repeatedly, perhaps throughout the years, and that you've never gotten around to looking up. For example, the Copenhagen Interpretation, what your employee purportedly has recently contracted and is out sick with, the latest club/activity/seminar you vaguely heard your spouse has signed you up to participate in, or if punk rock is still relevant. I keep a running list on my phone so the thought can move out and make room for the latest conundrum, such as the current millage rate for the county, the lifespan of the tussock moth caterpillar, and how long it would take to scull around the world with a suitable provision boat accompaniment if there were perfect weather conditions.

103 THINGS TO DO, Outside of Screaming Profanity, Self-Mutilation and Bodily Harm to Others, While Downloading

RESEARCH NOTES:

_____
_____
_____
_____
_____
_____
_____
_____
_____
_____
_____
_____
_____
_____
_____
_____
_____
_____
_____
_____
_____
_____
_____
_____
_____
_____
_____
_____

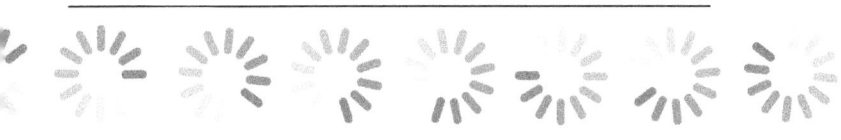

2. REPLACE BATTERIES IN EVERYTHING, EVERYWHERE.

Instead of purchasing a new product or gadget, which is my usual modus operandi but not the most cost effective approach just to avoid the tedium, replace all those batteries in your watches, smoke alarms, or whatever has been requiring them forever (watch those wireless keyboards they die at the most inopportune time). If this is a new experience for you, HowStuffWorks.com or Ehow.com may be informative. Something, somewhere, is begging to be brought back to life.

3. CLEAN YOUR IMMEDIATE SURROUNDINGS.

Granted someone else may be contracted or generously volunteers to do so, but give it a whirl. Improving your space and creating gratitude for the usual parties who do it—a 2-for-1! Buzzle.com offers a checklist and template for any that might be cleaning challenged. The site is flush with cleaning advice.

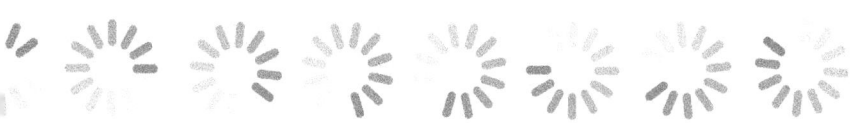

4. ASSESS YOUR ELECTRONIC POWER STRIPS (MODIFY AFTER YOU FINISH YOUR DOWNLOADING).

Mine look like snakes that met a lawnmower. Detangle them and check for tears or breaks. There is an interesting power strip that saves you money by stopping the vampire power effect. Since many of us don't shut the power strips off, Bits offers Smart Strips for thirty dollars (at the time of this publication). It could potentially save you up to fifty dollars a year, depending on how many strips you use and how much power strip policing you do or don't do. Be safe, change the strips, and possibly create a winner for the budget.

5. COMPUTER GAMES.

Who said this wasn't allowed? That is, unless the IT guys have disabled and blocked every conceivable joyous use for company technology. While some of you may work for the big tech firms, which provide everything from walking your dog to raising your children as employment perks, herein lies the purpose for carrying additional technology. Keep the noise to a minimum if you're in an office, and then you can look forward to downloading. In fact, you will be finding every reason to download every large and byte-sucking document you can justify. Downloading at home couldn't be more fun with your latest game technology nearby, unless your children happen to be busy with the same system.

6. MAKE A RANDOM ACT OF KINDNESS LIST.

An integrated norm for many and hopefully never cliché, at times by not thinking ahead we may miss great opportunities to help others. Keeping a list of ideas will keep the practice fresh. One acquaintance I know hands out dollar store packs of plastic rain ponchos occasionally during rainstorms to needy pedestrians. Try buying the purchases of the person next to you, or their meal, toll, beverage, ticket, or prescription, for a truly satisfying experience for everyone. Maybe the person in the next cube just needs their work off the central copy machine. If a face-to-face kindness encounter is too much for the shy types, try donations online, microloans like Kiva.org, or similar organizations (after carefully researching the organization or charity). M.J. Schrader wrote in an article that an act of kindness boosts your immune system, among other good physiological things.

103 THINGS TO DO, Outside of Screaming Profanity, Self-Mutilation and Bodily Harm to Others, While Downloading

RANDOM ACT OF KINDNESS IDEAS LIST:

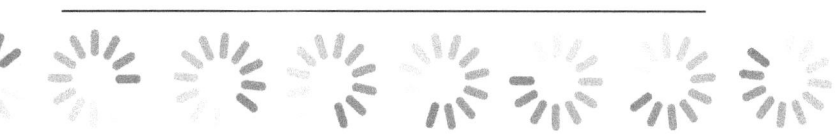

7. OPEN REGULAR SNAIL MAIL.

Yes, the stack that grows despite e-mail and attempts at going paperless. Who knew you were in line for winning the Publishers Clearing House Sweepstakes? The joy of surprises! I still carry a soft spot for the Postal Service (no e-mails please), and enjoyed reading about its history at about.usps.com. You know you'll miss those Saturday deliveries.

8. CALL YOUR PARENTS.

No explanation needed. Plus, when the download is complete, you have the perfect excuse to say goodbye. Remember, they will probably use that on you too sometime.

9. MAKE A TRAVEL LIST.

List places you want to visit, rating them with one (immediate), two (within the next couple of years), or three (going-to-do-it dream vacation destination). Research one of them and be brave—actually do it! Trade homes, exchange couch adventures, try youth hostels, volunteer for creative housing with work options with the national park system, mentally review any incredibly hospitable friends you might have met in the past ten years who you could impose upon, and make it happen. You can do it ASAP at HotelTonight.com, an online booking app with decent last-minute options. Then you can download in a really nice place.

103 THINGS TO DO, Outside of Screaming Profanity, Self-Mutilation and Bodily Harm to Others, While Downloading

TRAVEL WISH LIST:

10. READ A BOOK.

This may have been a common fallback in the past for any open moments and a given eons ago, but today, reading needs fresh marketing. Of course not to you, as you are reading this—*bravo*! Consult your favorite bibliophile for recommendations. In an effort to connect you with your technology, try Clive Thompson's *Smarter Than You Think—How Technology is Changing Our Mind for the Better*. It might improve your technology relationships despite their aggravating processes.

11. IN KEEPING WITH A SIMILAR THEME OF READING, TRY YOUR HAND AT POETRY.

Write anything, something, substance, or musings. Scratching out a thought might lead to words with forever, life-changing implications. Whether Haiku, lyric (adaptations to a new song, maybe?), ode, epigram, limerick, sonnet, etc., it's the effort that counts.

> Downloading....................................
> Despite the 85% complete line,
> I really doubt the completion time.
> Give me instant as nothing else will do,
> Otherwise count me blue.

Quality? Depth? No one said publish them.

12. LEARN A LANGUAGE.

There are myriads of options for language education with improved online routes and applications. In addition to adding to your skill set, it improves your memory capacities. You will also have the advantage of not having to choose between those phone options (press one for _____ or two for _____), as you'll know them both well, therefore eliminating irritating phone system prompts until they add more languages to the list. But hey, you have a lot of downloading, so bring it on!

13. SHINE YOUR SHOES.

Normally, who has the time? Who also has twenty dollars, tip not included, for the street/airport/shoe repair store person to do it? Pick up one of those little, cheap kits at the local department store to keep at your desk and get busy on those shoes you are wearing or those resting nearby. You'll be glad you did. Hero status for you if you do another person's shoes (provided you did not grab their feet and shoes arbitrarily).

14. STOP WHINING AND GRAB ANOTHER PIECE OF TECHNOLOGY.

Rarely are we without alternatives, such as a laptop, smartphone, tablet, e-reader, or borrowing another's technology, to get back to normal business while the other technology takes its sweet time to perform. In desperate moments I've used the public library. Don't soak in a pool of tech despair—go around the issue (a life lesson to live by?).

15. PAY THOSE LANGUISHING BILLS.

Whether it is online or old-style mail and checkbook, wrap up those lingering personal account payables and feel so efficient! Knocking them out even piecemeal makes them less of a burden. If you have been incredibly efficient and have up-to-date balanced books, consider making a healthy financial practice of checking your accounts daily to prevent hacking with your personal finances.

16. CLEAN YOUR TECHNOLOGY.

Not limiting it to just phone or computer screens (check out staywellkept.com with its fashionable wipes, they are impressive in business meetings and beats using your sleeve or shirt tail), try unclogging your charging ports, headphone jack, phone housing, and keyboards of dirt. SixWise.com states contamination of keyboards is prevalent, and most keyboards tested positive for a staph bacterium named coagulase (negative staphylococci), and 80 percent of keyboards contained diphtheriods. SixWise.com adds, "Keyboards may be successfully decontaminated with disinfectants." Refer to your operating manuals and, at your own risk, use common sense.

17. SKYPE A FRIEND/FAMILY/NECESSARY SOMEONE.

Why not dial up a friendly face instead of staring at the technology? Do not mention you are waiting on a download and remember to smile. Make the face time even if it's only for a moment. Someone out there is really looking forward to seeing the beautiful you!

18. BRUSH UP ON YOUR MEDIA MANNERS.

Of course you are the quintessential Miss Manners' protégé with perfect tweets and e-mails. Seriously, can you say with 100 percent accuracy that you know your tech manners? Want to bet your career on it? Emoticons at work—you tell me. And yes, there are opinions on it. In 2010, the Radicati Group estimated approximately 294 billion e-mails were sent. One can only imagine the e-mail growth to date, indicating a lot of communication that could use a bit of fine-tuning. You can also go to NetManners.com, a website dedicated to assisting people with their e-mails.

19. GROUPON/TIPPER/LIVING SOCIAL/ETC.

Peruse the latest and greatest offers of the day for a bargain. Ever buy one of those daily not-to-be-had-again specials and wish you had not? Relieve yourself of the unwanted load at Presentify.me by turning your purchase into a gift certificate to give away. Perhaps that four-hour introductory gator tracking experience for the entire family or that intended gift of lipo laser treatments for your best friend (who isn't anymore) were not the best of ideas.

20. WATER YOUR PLANTS, YOUR ASSOCIATE'S PLANTS, YOUR NEIGHBOR'S PLANTS, OR WHATEVER PLANTS ARE IN THE SURROUNDING AREA.

Playing among the green stuff is healthy for your lungs. You are receiving revitalizing oxygen from plants, which may help a bit with that short, shallow breathing that comes with the frustration of downloading. In addition to calming you, it will also show general goodwill with any onlookers, qualifying as an act of random kindness that will allow you to cross one off the to-do list for the day.

21. FILING.

Egads! We all need to do it, whether e-filing, accordion folders, or big antiquated f-i-l-i-n-g cabinets. It is nearly as fun as the download process, although it could be more exercise provided you stand up to do it. About.com/Small Business has suggestions on document management to speed up the process. An interesting app for organization in general is IFTTT.com. Desiring more interesting file folders? Try lillianvernon.com or currentcatalog.com to spice up your hard copy filing.

22. SAVE MONEY.

For every download, deposit a coin or a bill into a container, and voilà—practiced savings! Place a container nearby to collect the designated amount. I'm a dime-a-download type. Now, you can make this a very positive cue to turn around a negative experience. The spare change you collect can be your donation money or special treat fund, or you could also glue pennies to the floor. I recently saw it on a home improvement show, making for a very interesting floor covering. No question as to where that penny went!

23. PRACTICE BEING CHARMING.

Rasmussen reports in a poll (they poll just about everything) that 70 percent of Americans are getting ruder. I think this is in part due to excessive and incredible download times, but others think financial woes, healthcare issues, the housing crisis, job concerns, economy, and so on, not to mention the flat feet epidemic, could be the cause. Whatever the case may be, practicing charm is a life enhancing skill that leads to many positive outcomes. Eons ago, schools actually taught children such skills, along with parents. As adults who may have missed that training, it would behoove those like myself who are at times charm deficient to get our polish on for professional and personal improvement. Studies show it might increase your salary.

24. TEMPORARILY SUSPEND OR STOP THE DOWNLOAD.

If you can't fill the download time with something productive, then move on to something else and come back to that particular download later when you can leave the process alone. Building frustrations and downbeat attitudes won't lead to a constructive outcome, and they're not healthy. Return to the download at a time when it is manageable. Or let it go! Do we *really* need all this information?

CHAPTER 2
HEALTHY AND MEANINGFUL

25. DOODLE.

Research from the University of Plymouth indicates scribbling and scrawling may boost your brain's ability to notice and remember mundane information by 30 percent. Doodle away, getting all your creative juices flowing. For fun, go to Quibblo.com or Ask.com (there are others you can Google) and have your doodle analyzed.

103 THINGS TO DO, Outside of Screaming Profanity, 31
Self-Mutilation and Bodily Harm to Others, While Downloading

DOODLE AWAY

26. EXERCISE!

Of course that is the healthiest and most common stress reduction advice around. I feel exercise comes in a variety of forms; therefore, throwing the nearest object to a safe landing spot creates the appropriate arm movement involving weight and stretching exercises, along with improved hand-to-eye coordination. Be sure no one, including animals, is within throwing range unless you have superior aim. You cannot sue me should you overestimate your abilities. Beware of throwing your tech device—although warranted, it will only complicate matters.

27. SMILE.

Oh yes, you can do it! Research shows that by smiling, you encourage your entire being to be happier, causing internal changes that are beneficial, even if you really aren't happy. It's tricking the body, so to speak. Of course you're not happy, bordering on freaking crazy at times, while waiting for your download. Nevertheless, play the game, and you will profit. Especially if someone within proximity is deserving of your smile and willing to reciprocate. Be a starter, make the effort, and just smile.

28. BALANCE ON ONE FOOT, ALTERNATING FEET FOR THIRTY SECONDS.

For safety, please have a rail, chair, or very friendly person to hang onto until you are a balance master. Studies show you are going to lose your ability to balance, especially on one foot with your eyes closed, as you age. While you might not think that is a horrible loss, it relates to your entire body becoming less agile. It's one small step to a broken hip before you know it. Stop the loss now, and go to LiveStrong.com or ShareCare.com, among many others, for guidance on balance.

29. ACUPRESSURE FACELIFT.

It is reported that you can give those bothersome wrinkles a good-bye wave if you faithfully practice facial acupressure exercises. Search for the exercise chart online or go to acupuncture-austin.com for directions on a five minute acupressure face lift. Post them near your computer and take those extra seconds/minutes/hours to renew your face. It can't hurt to try and costs less than surgery if it succeeds—that's what I'm telling myself.

30. CLEAR YOUR HEAD.

Downloading comes with a semi-truck full of bad thoughts. With all those negative considerations swimming through your neural pathways, you might want to rid yourself of the especially frightful ones. Author Richard Petty, PhD, professor of psychology at Ohio State, indicated that you can shed destructive thoughts by writing them down on a piece of paper and then tossing it away. He states you will be less swayed or influenced by the thought after doing this. It's an excellent idea if violence and self-loathing pop into your mind while you wait prone on the floor during downloads, writhing in anguish and contemplating unpleasant alternatives.

31. CHEW GUM (QUIETLY).

Gum chewing stimulates the brain as it works off excess frustrations, similar to exercise; it is the oral kind. It helps with dieting as well, so think of it as a 3-for-1 if you chew the peppermint xylitol-sweetened kind. It is great for oral health due to its abilities to reduce acid-producing bacteria. It also has the added benefit of peppermint, which is mentally stimulating and aids with digestion. Serious caveat—xylitol is reported to be toxic to dogs, so be sure to keep your gum away from your canine friends.

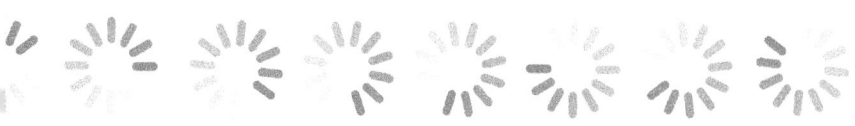

32. MUSIC.

Find the playlist of sixty beats per minute music to use during downloading. The sixty beats per minute will calm you, and it is said that it is better for you than a massage. I wouldn't go that far, but it is worthwhile. Enter "sixty beats per minute music" on your favorite music tech device for suggestions. YouTube also will offer you very nice options.

33. EAT DARK CHOCOLATE AND WALNUTS.

It turns out that they are feel-good foods. Walnuts contain valuable omegas and tryptophan, which your body uses to create serotonin. Dark chocolate, according to FitDay.com, may lower blood pressure and harden tooth enamel, and it "contains phenylethylamine (PEA), the same chemical your brain creates when you feel like you're falling in love. PEA encourages your brain to release endorphins, so eating dark chocolate will make you feel happier." Why wait for downloading periods? It's a healthy nosh for any occasion, so long as you remember portion control.

34. EAR RUB.

University of Connecticut researchers indicated that squeezing or rubbing the exterior of the earlobe stimulates acupressure points and may create a happier mood, in addition to cutting food cravings. No claims here; I'm only passing along the information, and rubbing my ear while envisioning weight loss. Do try to be careful, and if you go gorilla on your ear, at the very least you will have a new issue to worry about besides downloads.

35. COMMENSURATE.

The ladies know this one well, but men have a harder time with commiserating unless it comes with a sports score or motor woe of some sort. Britain's University of Lancaster research demonstrated that expressing and sharing our frustrations with co-workers and others releases stress and creates better bonds. It is suggested to stay with the subject matter of downloading as opposed to your boss and his or her shortcomings, unless you'd like to add joblessness to your list of complaints.

36. TOSS A BALL IN THE AIR.

No ball? Use a pen, cup, or any loose object. Playing catch is a skill that will serve you well over a lifetime, in all probability you will be required to catch items quite a lot. Beyond sports, falling items from a cabinet, your children, an ill person (where were you when I did a face-to-floor meeting in the checkout line?), your pet, tree fruit, a tipsy friend, possibly an elderly person, and you may even need to catch yourself. A little catch training could be beneficial use of your time. Don't believe me? YouTube funny catch classics and see a very awesome dad catching his child from a swing.

37. CRY, CRY, CRY, BABY!

Janis Joplin got it right—a good cry is immeasurably worth it. Of course, your immediate environment dictates your ability to do so. In your office cube or during a business meeting certainly makes this less of an option; however, if you are out of earshot and alone, have at it. NetDoctor.com states there are multiple advantages to crying, from removing toxins to uplifting our moods. Some of us are well-versed in crying and consider it a practiced art. For those of you who aren't, instead of a long download, imagine a computer crash or a ruined hard drive with no backup, then reach for the tissues and begin your wail.

38. DANCE.

Dancing incorporates many healthy suggestions into one: physical activity, mental stimulation, and relaxing music. Of course your body is probably considered only physically doodling because most of us cannot dance (you know it's true). Proficient or not, dancing also increases cognitive activity in all ages, writes Richard Powers, who quotes from the *New England Journal of Medicine*. Dancing was cited as the greatest risk reduction of any activity studied, cognitive or physical, for protection against dementia as we age. With or without music, let your body move.

103 THINGS TO DO, Outside of Screaming Profanity, Self-Mutilation and Bodily Harm to Others, While Downloading

39. HAVE A GLASS OF WINE (PROVIDED YOU ARE OF DRINKING AGE AND NOT AT WORK).

Do so especially if the downloaded material involves an attorney, taxes, or an ex-spouse. A glass of wine, particularly red wine, according to HealthCentral.com, has anti-inflammatory properties and has been found to help prevent heart attacks and increase the amount of HDL (good cholesterol). What's more, it contains flavonoids, which can help prevent cancer and decrease the chances of blood clotting. Of course you can't drink on the job, but you can reserve this pleasure for after work to reward yourself for your downloading patience. Hopefully a full bottle is not necessary, though.

40. PRAY.

Pray with thankfulness and gratitude that you don't have to download all day and that you have technology to download with (you know, people still don't have fresh water in this world somewhere, let alone smartphones, tablets, and computers). Pray for forgiveness for all involved; I don't know who or where they are that contribute to the software and cyber download experience, but ask for mercy for all involved. Begging for patience is another good idea. Seriously, a silent moment for prayer would be considered a beautiful opportunity. We all need divine help.

41. SCALP MASSAGE.

University of Miami research reported that by massaging your scalp, you can cut stress hormones from one to three hours—essentially, one download. It also wakes up those hair follicles by increasing circulation and blood flow potentially helping with hair growth. No willing assistant? DIY, folks. You can go to Amazon.com, which offers those scalp ticklers for five dollars plus outrageous shipping unless you add on.

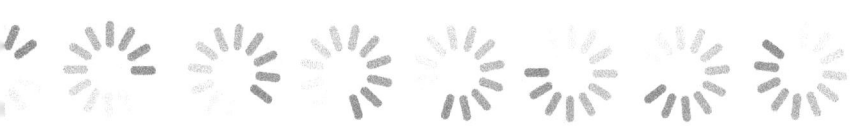

42. YOUTUBE A PET VIDEO.

Watching animals has positive effects, so YouTube the latest cute pet video. My favorite is Animal Planet's *Too Cute* series for a mind-crushing, work warrior day. The video pace alone is a chill factor. Megan Garber writes in *The Atlantic*, "In a study from Hiroshima University, scientists examined the effects of animals' cuteness—termed kawaii—on human behavior." The researchers conducted three experiments to determine those effects, measuring subject cognition, and the surprisingly good news is that people who looked at pictures of cute baby animals outperformed those who did not. Even more intriguing, they outperformed people who looked at pictures of only adult animals. Enough said. Check out YouTube baby animals and stop making fun of those who do, because they could quite possibly outperform you.

43. PUNCH A PILLOW OR ANY SOFT OBJECT.

LiveStrong.com endorses the practice, stating "symbolically you may picture the punching bag or pillow as a representation of your stress. Imagining a troublesome situation or person in your life and punching at the bag allows you to express anger in a healthier way to becoming physical with another person." I'd add computer as well. It could also keep you out of jail.

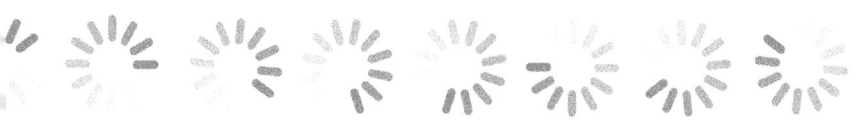

44. PUT TOGETHER A SAFETY PLAN.

In this day and age of unprecedented violence and catastrophes, arrange an emergency plan for you and your family in case of mass shootings, home invasions, carjackings, assaults, and, sadly, so on. Making a list of how you and your family need to prepare and react to these incidents could save lives and ease communications if unfortunate situations arise. Listing important numbers elsewhere in case you are without your personal cell, creating code words within your family and trusted neighbors to signal alarm, storing away credit card numbers in case of loss, and mapping out exit routes in the home or at work are all areas to address, as well as many others. Our daily lives are so full, we often neglect or put off making preparations with the thought that it could never happen us. For neighborhood communication, a useful website is NextDoor.com

103 THINGS TO DO, Outside of Screaming Profanity, Self-Mutilation and Bodily Harm to Others, While Downloading

SAFETY PLAN ACTIONS:

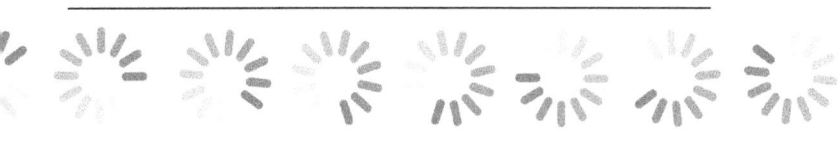

45. MEMORIES.

Try recalling a wonderful memory, anything that brought you joy. A British study found it changes your mood instantly, approximately 15 percent more than the previous suggestion of smiling. Pleasure is the flower that passes; remembrance, the lasting perfume ~ Jean de Boufflers. Be determined to make worthwhile memories, then take them out for review and reflection now and then.

46. GET ON THE FLOOR AND CRAWL.

Crawling in adults engages right-side brain activity. Ohashiatsu.org states that due to our "linear thinking and computer skills in today's technological society, we aren't developing both sides of our brain." By crawling and increasing right-side brain actions, improvements occur in memory, balance, vision, and mental clarity. Caveat—unless you are near children or pets who will jump at the chance to join you, do this in a private setting. Stuck at the office? Pretend to be looking for something. On the other hand, doing this frequently in an office setting could get you a human resources referral to the optometrist or psychiatrist.

47. DO A QUICK LAYMAN'S ORAL CHECKUP.

Go to the nearest restroom with a mirror and view your tongue and teeth. How often do you do that? See any red flags? Call for an appointment now! The Mayo Clinic states that oral health is a window to your overall health and is more important than you may realize. It has connections to cardiovascular disease and other conditions.

48. GO OUTSIDE OR AT LEAST SIT NEAR A SUNNY WINDOW.

Robin Elton wrote at SimpleGreenOrganicHappy.com that sunshine exposure is critical to your daily vitamin D dose. Proper vitamin D levels boost calcium absorption for strong bones, protect eye health, and boost your immunity. The article added that sunshine lowers blood pressure and reduces stroke risk. Lastly, it mentions being able to sleep better since the sun regulates circadian rhythms, along with overall improving your mood. A dose of vitamin D and a bit of natural warmth sure beats pacing back and forth in front of the computer.

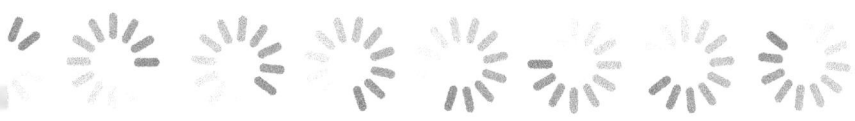

49. DRINK A GLASS OF WATER.

Benefits—let me count the ways. Top of the list is zero calories! It fills you up with no penalties, only boosting your metabolism. Did you know dehydration can mask itself as hunger, causing us to overeat? Dehydration can also result in a headache. Water removes toxins, keeping our interior clean and our system regulated. It refreshes you, restores your energy, and normalizes your body temperature. The list could go on! Just know that it is a wonderfully healthy habit at all times, download break or not.

50. CLOSE YOUR EYES AND TAKE AN EYELID REST.

Mind you, not a serious nap because someone, somewhere, is waiting for a response from you on that download. Shut your eyes and briefly rest (Dr. Oz suggests ten minutes) or watch those spots—eye floaters—dash about. In case you were wondering, Mark Stibich, PhD, states in Tips for Great Naps, ""The primetime naptime is from 1:00 p.m. to 3:00 p.m., when your energy level dips due to a rise in the hormone melatonin at that time of day."" Since you download all the time, set an alarm for no more than ten to twenty minutes so you don't slip into a stage three or four deep sleep, which will leave you feeling groggy and tired.

51. PLAY WITH A PET.

Beyond watching a video, try a real moment with a pet. Engaging with a pet is an instant stress reducer, providing the pet does not bite, isn't dirty, doesn't have a communicable disease, and is not virtual. Virtual anything doesn't count. Virtuals are a tech illusion, built on assumed realities made to appear significant. Playing with a real pet reduces anxiety, dropping the level of cortisol while increasing serotonin production. One study indicated that it can also lower your blood pressure. *USA Today* wrote that a study published in the spring of 2012, led by Randolph Barker, showed stress level scores fell about 11 percent among workers who brought their dogs to work, while stress increased 70 percent for those who did not. There is a national Take Your Dog to Work Day, started in 1999 by Pet Sitters International, which is celebrated on the Friday following Father's Day. Work that into your next employment package.

52. WHISTLE.

Remember whistling as a child? It really is fun, at least for the person doing it, although not necessarily for those who hear it unless you're very good at it. There are health benefits to whistling as well. It's great exercise for the lungs and proper breath control. Remember the "Whistle While You Work" song in Disney's *Snow White and the Seven Dwarfs* animated movie? They were onto something. Rollingstone.com lists their picks of the fifteen best whistling songs of all time.

53. CHANGE YOUR PASSWORDS.

My employer requires that I do it at work regularly, repeatedly, and annoyingly more often than I care to. Doing so before I get the notice gives me perverse pleasure of being ahead of the game. I've carried the practice over to my personal accounts. This cuts down on hacking and privacy invasion. Mind you, my password refresh list is a novel in itself.

103 THINGS TO DO, Outside of Screaming Profanity, Self-Mutilation and Bodily Harm to Others, While Downloading

SCRATCH PAGE FOR PASSWORD CHANGES:

54. SCHEDULE APPOINTMENTS.

Downloading moments are the perfect time to schedule appointments. Appointments abound in work and personal life alike; add in those for family members, and you practically need a personal assistant to cover this base. Stop gloating, those of you who do. Thankfully, most firms are working with online calendar systems, so picking up the phone is becoming unnecessary. Churn out those cable company/doctor/dentist/barber/salon/contractor/auto repair/seminar/registration/meeting/etc., appointments and feel oh so organized instead of agonized.

55. YAWN.

Do a big one, really wide, a couple of times. It brings oxygen to the brain. You'll need it once the download finishes, allowing you to move along with the task at hand. Please be polite and cover your mouth. In a dog training class, I was told yawning in dogs at times is a sign of anxiety. I am sure downloading yawns in us humans could qualify too.

56. WASH YOUR HANDS.

How much stuff do we touch, not to mention people we shake hands with, throughout the day? Maybe it is only your child or pet, but, nevertheless, washing hands is critical to remaining healthy. We do it less these days, depending on hand sanitizers that are scattered wherever we go (who is sanitizing the sanitizers?). Statistics support hand washing over hand sanitizers, plus your nails are left cleaner and neater. Called the DIY vaccine, the Centers for Disease Control (CDC) recommends twenty seconds of lathering as the guideline.

57. STRETCH.

How many people really do this? Different from exercise, which builds muscle, stretching lengthens the muscle. It is a health essential, and even your arteries notice if you don't do it. *Body+Soul* stated a study at the University of Illinois found that when people followed a regular stretching program, they experienced a boost in their self-esteem. It appears stretching releases dopamine, which helps you feel happier and more positive about the world, says Dr. Simon, chiropractor and ambassador for Allied Health and Prevention. Go to one of those apps or online websites to show you great stretching moves that can be done at your desk and don't always require activities on the floor.

58. WALK BACKWARD.

Kangaroos and emus actually cannot, and the Japanese, purportedly, love walking backward because it burns more calories than walking forward. Studies show that walking backward reduces the force on our knees and is useful for anyone experiencing pain while going up and down stairs or doing lunges or squats. It takes more energy, thereby burning more calories, and helps with balance. While I don't suggest doing it publicly, check out the YouTube video "Tokyo Reverse." It is a highlight reel from a nine-hour video of a person walking backward, with very interesting video work.

59. RAKE A ZEN GARDEN.

The manufacturers market them as a relaxation device. Ever get one of those as an office gift? Ever break one? A passing thought would be to be thankful you are not raking a real yard. They say raking does calm the mind, so miniature or not, it is an option. Next time, ask for a cactus as a gift. The plant, according to certain sources, helps absorb radiation from your old-style computer monitor. While some websites debate that point, HealthMad.com offers a variety of tips that include a cactus to prevent computer radiation. Of course, you could always justify new technology, which is greener and healthier these days (thank you Apple).

60. ROLL YOUR EYES.

This ought to be easy since it's a natural frustration reaction, possibly bringing you back to your juvenile days and authority encounters. Actually, it is a valid exercise that strengthens your eyes and improves your vision, reducing stress and potentially improving dry eyes. It is truly advantageous if you've been staring at the computer in a wishful if not insistent state, watching and willing the download to complete. Eyestrain is not good. Now you have the time to correct it.

61. SQUEEZE A TENNIS BALL.

Would you like to lower blood pressure and create a better grip at the same time? The American Heart Association states this exercise caused a reduction in blood pressure. Further, by squeezing the ball for several seconds, you increase the strength of your hand. You can envision squeezing the computer as if you could hasten downloading, squeezing every last byte out *quickly*!

62. HAND MASSAGE.

Speaking of hands, take a moment to massage yours, top and bottom. A hand and foot reflexology chart can be found at Acupressure.com, diagramming important meridian points. Simply massaging your hand can open up stagnant meridians and increase alertness. You may also increase alertness by gently slapping the inside of your wrist. Go to WebMD.com for other suggestions on staying alert and awake while waiting for downloads.

63. TAKE A RESTROOM BREAK.

So simple, and yet I'm reminding you.

64. IMPROVE YOUR COMPUTER SPACE.

Move your monitor for optimum distance for eyesight and head angle. Adjust your chair, especially if you share your space with another shift or family, to maximize comfort and afford proper posture. Declutter the area, disposing of old hard-copy paper reminders, broken items, and unused objects that no longer, or never did, serve a useful purpose (I've reserved a roll-off dumpster). Now perk it up! You might add aromatherapy (rosemary, orange, and peppermint are stimulating and focusing), refresh or repaint the walls (soothing yet centering colors), or try installing instant on capabilities for all your devices so they engage when you enter the area. Maybe it is time to purchase or make that request of your employer for a new ergonomic chair or other products.

CHAPTER 3

WHATEVER AND FOR WHAT IT IS WORTH

65. EXPLETIVES.

Count the expletives that come to your mind that you will refrain from saying. Vow to expand your vocabulary. Need help? Look up CussControl.com.

103 THINGS TO DO, Outside of Screaming Profanity, Self-Mutilation and Bodily Harm to Others, While Downloading

66. THUMB FIGHT.

Actually thumb wrestling, not to be confused with the ancient art (no substantiation of that statement whatsoever) predating the computer game, can be played with a workmate, friend, relative, stranger (maybe you really are that charming), or, most importantly, solo. For rules and regulations, including instructions, check out eHow.com on thumb wrestling. An added thrill would be to beat your non-dominant hand.

67. EXCUSES.

Collect excuses from various people, organizations, departments, and any others who are remotely responsible for not being able to complete a download. Warning—this could result in volumes. I'll be looking for your book on Amazon.com; it should be quite entertaining.

68. HAIL A CAB.

For all the nonmetro/rural/small town dwellers, it is a real skill. You may never intend on going to a big city, but it can happen when you least expect it. My initial tries were pitiful and futile, while I watched my amused city-dwelling sister do it with ease. Don't be caught without the proper cab hailing skills. Travel.Yahoo.com has a nice pictorial on the entire process. Brandishing weapons is an obvious no-no.

69. MAKE A NEW ACRONYM LIST.

Oh yes, we need more acronyms in our lives. At the current rate of abbreviation, due to truncated communications, I fear the English language may soon be one big language cesspool of odd letters, guesstimates of their former words. Why not join the game and make some of your friends' favorite activities, then start confusing them by using them in e-mails, texts, and tweets. Wait a sufficient time to respond, letting the confusion sink deep as you spread the frustration. Enjoy the reactions of those who thought they knew what you were talking about but really didn't. Not creative? Then go to AcronymFinder.com and choose from over four million they have logged.

103 THINGS TO DO, Outside of Screaming Profanity, 79
Self-Mutilation and Bodily Harm to Others, While Downloading

ACRONYM LIST:

_____
_____
_____
_____
_____
_____
_____
_____
_____
_____
_____
_____
_____
_____
_____
_____
_____
_____
_____
_____
_____
_____
_____
_____
_____
_____
_____

70. TIME THE DOWNLOAD.

For comparison's sake, time it and keep a record. It may be an exercise that actually proves helpful since our perceptions rarely match our realities.

103 THINGS TO DO, Outside of Screaming Profanity, Self-Mutilation and Bodily Harm to Others, While Downloading

DOWNLOAD RECORD:

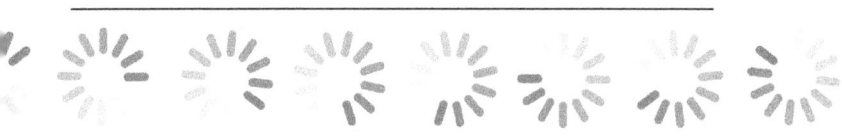

71. CHECK YOUR STOCK PRICES, INVESTMENTS, OR BANK BALANCE.

By frequently checking your financial condition, including credit score, it will lead to more informed and financially healthy decisions. Additionally, it may help with privacy issues, such as stolen identity and hacked accounts, by early detection. No comment on whether it will reduce the stress, but at least it will serve to take your mind off the download.

103 THINGS TO DO, Outside of Screaming Profanity, Self-Mutilation and Bodily Harm to Others, While Downloading

FINANCIAL TO DO LIST:

72. CREATE A LIST OF QUESTIONS TO STUMP YOUR LANGUAGE-DRIVEN TECHNOLOGY.

Of course, you have found normal requests easily do that too. This list is the crazy stuff you wonder about and know there really is no answer to. It is harder than you think, yet it always happens on simple things during a crunch time issue when Siri, Iris, Maluuba or Skyvi just don't get it. So play the game with them for real. It is also a look into those coders' minds with their weird, I mean really awesome, responses.

103 THINGS TO DO, Outside of Screaming Profanity, Self-Mutilation and Bodily Harm to Others, While Downloading

QUESTIONS:

_____
_____
_____
_____
_____
_____
_____
_____
_____
_____
_____
_____
_____
_____
_____
_____
_____
_____
_____
_____
_____
_____
_____
_____
_____
_____
_____

73. SPITTING CONTEST.

Yes, I said it. This ought to wake up those who have lost focus at this point. It can be done quite discreetly, as it is a personal contest (as seen on a recent late evening outing – who knew?). Head to the nearest restroom, aim at the sink or toilet, and try to beat your personal best. You know the expression "spitting mad", as in "I was spitting-mad the download failed five times before actually completing" —now you at least have an outlet for it.

74. LISTEN TO SOMEONE.

We all want to express ourselves and be heard, yet when it comes to listening, we rarely enjoy that side of the conversation as much. Research indicates we remember only between 24–50 percent of what the other person has said. "Be swift about hearing, slow about speaking, slow about wrath," according to James 1:19. Improving our listening skills is important, and it takes practice. Leave the downloading (including your cell phone), approach someone, engage in conversation while looking them in the eye, and concentrate on what they are saying. It is a gift of kindness to give your time and really just listen.

75. PAPER FOLDING.

With over fourteen million web search results, including origami, you can see the popularity of this option. I consider my elementary paper planes as far as I can take it. It truly is a well-defined ability. Maybe it's time to upgrade your paper folding and bring someone a little surprise. Who knows, what you fold could become the basis for a new idea or prototype and you will be bound for QVC or As Seen on TV.

76. VOICE MAIL MESSAGE.

Compose a voice mail greeting that is complicated, with as many prompts as you can think of, and put it on your personal phone. Compete with a friend and see whose message gets the most hang-ups. Come to think of it, isn't this what some major companies do as a rule for their automated phone systems now?

77. WATCH THE DOWNLOAD.

Those little circles, dashes, dots, arrows, and streaming lines are all mesmerizing, leading you to a meditative state. At least that's what someone was hoping. A few of them have cute little messages, percentages, time countdowns, and so forth. You can buy into it and naïvely trust your technology to be telling you the absolute truth. I strongly suggest not holding your breath.

78. BUILD YOUR DREAM HOUSE, GARDEN, NEW OFFICE LAYOUT, OR OTHER REAL ESTATE DREAM.

There are a variety of online design tools to facilitate your vision—FloorPlanner.com, Squidoo.com, HomeStyler.com, and MyTurnstone.com, to name a few. Have fun creating and recreating until you have the ideal model.

79. MEMORIZE THE COLOR WHEEL.

This will come in extremely handy, with a broad application. Based on this newfound information, you can dress, design, and decorate better, including impressing your graphics buddies. You can even take it further by memorizing the contrasting complementary color!

80. MAKE A PAPER CLIP NECKLACE.

Okay, no necklace—just join them together and fold them carefully back in the box. Once completed, place it in the supply closet or your cube mate's desk drawer. This iconic office supply necessity was William Middleborrk's patented product. Over a century old, the original design remains to this day and is available in every imaginable color. Amaze your friends with that paper clip trivia after you watch the next person try to pull out one from the box, only to get the entire box.

81. ATTEMPT TO READ BACKWARD.

You know how you've gotten those e-mail forwards with all the vowels left out and how you rate genius status because you can read it? Like everyone can't? Try reading backward, and then you can truly strut your stuff or change careers to be a proofreader.

82. ENTER CONTESTS.

There are many websites that direct you to current contests. At About.com, Sandra Gruschopf states it takes patience, perseverance, and a positive attitude to win. Well, now, who doesn't have those in extra supply? Honestly, it can't hurt to try while your technology is spinning its cyber web. You'll win something one day with enough entries, so state the professional contest entrants. Maybe even new technology that narrows and lessens the downloading encounters.

83. KEEP A DOWNLOAD LOG.

Note what, when, and how long the downloading took, then place that information in a spreadsheet. It might give you a measurable view of your downloading activity. You will be able to analyze what works, what wastes your time, which sources are known trouble, and what to avoid in the future. Try to let go of the thought of how much time you are spending with another mundane, exasperating task in life. To help with your scratch pad, knockknockstuff.com can supply you with incredibly humorous sticky notes, log and journaling books, along with funny note pads such as Why I'm in a Really, Really, Really Bad mood pad. You need only to check a box and inform the world. Downloading should be at the top of the list on that pad.

103 THINGS TO DO, Outside of Screaming Profanity, Self-Mutilation and Bodily Harm to Others, While Downloading   97

DOWNLOAD LOG:

84. CHECK FOR RECALLS.

If you aren't a news junkie, you may not know that your packaged food, child's toy, the car you are driving or practically any other manufactured item has been recalled. Go to recall.gov for current listings. It may be a minor issue but note certain recalls have been life threatening. Better safe than sorry as they say.

85. DAYDREAM.

Some people purposely slice out time to do it. Downloading affords you this opportunity for a nice mental mini vacation. Sabah Karimi wrote that it improved creativity, lowered blood pressure, boosted your mood, led to brainstorming new ideas, and improved your memory. Instead of outside sources creeping into your gray matter, allow your unengaged mind to wander freely.

86. COMPOSE AN ENCOURAGING NOTE TO SOMEONE WHO COULD USE A BOOST OR A LITTLE CHEER.

On the professional side, the note could be to a potential client or work associate. Personally, an encouraging note or e-mail to family or friends could make their day. Why not send a congratulatory e-mail to yourself for not breaking your technology during a download? You really are a self-controlled, admirable person, even if only for the moment. Seriously, you could send encouraging e-mails to yourself pre-meetings to pump you up, post-event to remind you the time wasn't fully wasted or pre-rough-annual-anniversary date (death of family member, friend, etc.) to keep yourself grounded and on track.

103 THINGS TO DO, Outside of Screaming Profanity, 101 Self-Mutilation and Bodily Harm to Others, While Downloading

THOUGHTS FOR NOTES:

87. SHOP.

Of course you can! Who doesn't need the latest tech gadget or a new pair of shoes? At the very least you could comparison shop for an upcoming purchase or splurge. If shopping is your anathema to a simplified life (the best course, no kidding), do grocery shopping online. What a relief to have it delivered to your doorstep or make a pickup so you don't have to battle the crowds.

88. FACEBOOK AND OTHER SOCIAL MEDIA HOUSECLEANING.

For all you popular people who are not worried about identity theft nor the media fingerprint you are leaving forever, check your following and maybe, just maybe, clear away a few of your closest 500+ friends. ScientificAmerica.com says being a social butterfly has an upside, but note that psychologist Robin Dunbar, in a New York Times article, stated people can only cognitively deal with about 150 friends to feel connected and not become overwhelmed. It's kind of like cleaning out a closet—a little tough to do but required at times.

89. CHECK THE CALENDAR FOR THE CELEBRATION OF THE DAY.

There is a national day for nearly anything you can imagine. I am particularly fond of the food related ones like Doughnut Day or Go Fishing Day (I just watch), and try not to miss celebrating. There are others that will amuse and equally confuse. Various websites show a variety of options. I reference NationalDayCalandar.com but am open to others in the event that one lists a Stay in Bed All Day celebration. The question is, when will they be adding a national Downloading Day? Imagine everyone downloading immense documents all day long, crashing servers and computers—ouch! For the time being, I'll set my sights on the next national Chocolate Chip Cookie Day.

90. DECORATE YOUR COMPUTER.

No, I am not joking. Check it out—they actually sell computer jewelry. I make no judgments here. While I abstain from the jewelry, I do admit to a little stuffed camel hanging out on top of one of my personal monitors. He's been flung far and wide during intense moments, and he keeps on smiling!

91. LINKEDIN.

It is a useful professional networking site and joining may open opportunities for you. If you are a member how often do you experience people endorsing you and contacting you, but you lack the time to reciprocate? Take a moment to return their interest and make your own endorsements. Update your contacts and search out lost ones to reconnect with professionally. In this instance, professional contacts cannot be too large, and a large list of endorsements are a plus. You never know when someone is searching for your talents, and that one special contact may help change your professional life.

92. GIFT CARDS.

At times you can find yourself pleasantly abundant with them and not necessarily interested in redeeming them with the issuer. There are gift card exchange websites that will help you unload the cards before they expire or you lose them, such as CardCash.com, GiftCardGranny.com, CardHub.com, and GiftCardRescue.com. Even if you choose to keep them, try logging your card numbers or upload them to an app like GoWallet or Gyft for added security.

93. TRACK A SHARK.

Feel like you swim with a few sharks at work? Watch the real ones navigate the seas at FishTrack.com or others. While you can't control the land sharks, you can take a break and look at the migratory patterns and behaviors of a mako or great white.

94. WRITE REVIEWS.

One of the nicest, and most disturbing, offshoots of our global web is the wide variety of opinions. At their best, reader reviews on products, services, music, doctors, companies, destinations, and activities are informative and useful. My purchases, motel/hotel stays, and restaurant choices are now predicated on the opinions and experiences of others. It has been working quite well for years. When writing a review, try to be thorough, descriptive, and detailed. "Love it" or "awesome" does not indicate its quality or whether it performed/tasted great/turned out as expected. Explain why you can't live without it, hate it, regifted it, trashed it, returned it (how did that go?), or otherwise. You will find many people eager for your thoughts, but don't be surprised if your review gets reviewed, rebutted, recanted, or challenged. You have to take the good with the bad in the process.

95. MAKE A LIST OF ALL THE THINGS THAT YOU LOVE TO DO THAT ARE FREE.

Include things that are free to do, things that are free to enjoy, and anything free that brings you happiness. If you want to expand your list, web search what is free to do in your town or your favorite places, and you might find great suggestions to try. Life's daily experiences bring new insights and opportunities, so revise and review this list frequently.

103 THINGS TO DO, Outside of Screaming Profanity, Self-Mutilation and Bodily Harm to Others, While Downloading

FREE THINGS I LOVE TO DO OR WANT TO DO LIST:

_____
_____
_____
_____
_____
_____
_____
_____
_____
_____
_____
_____
_____
_____
_____
_____
_____
_____
_____
_____
_____
_____
_____
_____
_____
_____
_____

96. CLAP YOUR HANDS.

Add a beat and sing your favorite clapping song ("If you're happy and you know it, clap your hands" or Pharrell's "Happy") either out loud or in your head. Consider it your personal applause for enduring downloading. If someone notices, you can attribute it to them, applauding their latest great deed. wikiHow.com has a "how to clap hands," explaining different styles and purposes. I am adding that to my list of worries—how to clap and why.

97. TAKE A PICTURE.

Not the popular "selfie" or you sprawled out appearing comatose while draped over your computer, which would not be appreciated by your employer, but actual interesting objects, places, or people within your vicinity. If you use your cell phone, look into the apps that will improve your shots, like Camera+, Camera Zoom FX, and others. You never know what interesting candid shots could actually be exposed. What your mind and camera eye eventually rest upon could be a surprise to you and others. Take a look at Kate Hutchinson's work. FYI - according to the 2013 Direct Line survey, 90 percent of dog owners take more pictures of their pets than of their partners. You might try branching out.

98. GIVE SPELLING A CHANCE.

If you thought spelling bees were only for children, guess again. There are national adult spelling bee competitions, including the AARP National Senior Spelling Bee (something to work toward). For those who are a whiz with words, why not take these downloading moments and put them to good use with vocabulary builders and memory programs that you can parlay into competitive spelling. It would also improve your word gaming.

99. OPTIMIZE AND UPGRADE.

Buy new technology, increase your broadband, upgrade your Internet connection, limit your downloads to one at a time, enhance your computer, visit an internet website for a speed test, and Google/Bing/Chrome/Yahoo/Ask.com/whatever to see what new ideas have been developed and are being shared.

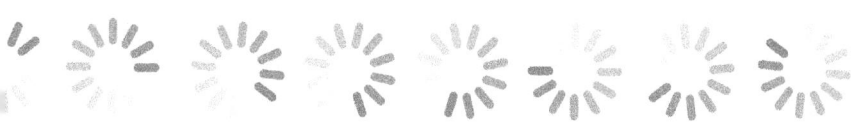

100. JOURNAL.

Capture your amazing thoughts with journaling, creating a snapshot in time of recollections and thoughts. My father had an interesting career in the space industry and recounts many stories that I wish had been recorded so the details and other experiences were not lost. Whatever you are doing now, you may want to recall it with vivid, written proof versus fuzzy memories. The benefits of journaling are numerous, listed by others to assist with increased focus, stress relief, release of pent up thoughts and emotions, and improved problem-solving skills.

103 THINGS TO DO, Outside of Screaming Profanity, Self-Mutilation and Bodily Harm to Others, While Downloading

JOURNAL THOUGHTS OR IDEAS:

101. ADD TO YOUR GREEN INITIATIVES.

In addition to your normal recycling and repurposing efforts and energy saving measures, up the ante and find new ways to improve your environment. Check out the sustainability industry's expanding ideas. See if you can incorporate new products (letsgogreen.biz, greenbuildingadvisor.com) and latest ideas (greenbiz.com), or invest in up-and-coming sustainable companies. Don't minimize the impact that you can make.

102. APPS AND APP MANAGEMENT.

The scores of apps that exist are incredible, and more are being developed at any given moment. They educate, entertain (everyone else within earshot too), assist in delightful ways, and at times shock us. I tend to shop apps weekly, looking for the latest and greatest. It is amazing what can be found, which brings me to the second portion of this—app management. Downloading could be the perfect time to delete and reevaluate our app selections. Whether a low-expectation review steers me wrong, the app does not work well with my technology, or I grow tired of it, I eliminate it to make way for the new. PCMag.com and TechCrunch.com, one of my favorite daily reads, can also offer insights on apps.

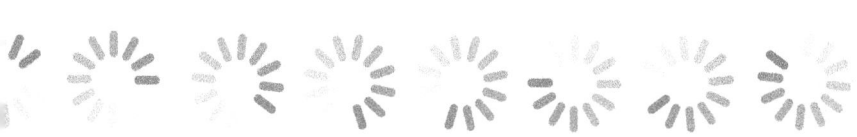

103. WORK.

Now there's a novel thought! Instead of fixating on the downloading and its connection to whatever it is you're working on, work on another component of the project or change projects. Shift your focus to other aspects of work. "My grandfather once told me that there were two kinds of people: those who do the work and those who take the credit. He told me to try to be in the first group; there was much less competition," said Indira Gandhi.

IN CONCLUSION

While contemplating downloading (oops, idea 104) during downloading, it occurred to me that maybe the computer, tablet, smartphone, e-reader, whatever-new technology eyeglasses, watches, and tomorrow's next best thing are not trying to download at all. They are taking a technical break because they have the capabilities - not the right, mind you - but the ability to do it. It's a true conspiracy, one that Hollywood has yet to depict onscreen. All those IT wizards who bang out software code with incredible instant gratification features actually create long downloads with extensive periods of waiting in order to generate brief bursts of relief and then happiness for the end user. It teaches us a lesson that

we do not get it all in life, and a suck-it-up measure is needed to keep us grounded (and nearly insane, simultaneously).

As a final thought to downloading, try acquiescence, knowing that things could always be worse. You could lose your job, you could break both legs, your car engine could blow, your investments could tank, your plumbing system could fail in the middle of a cold night, your dog could start to bite you only, your mattress could become a rat's residence, or you could contract a fatal disease—you know where this is going. I'd like to think there is an amount of acceptance to be had from downloading. It's one of those processes, like standing in line, teeth cleaning, and long-winded conversations from your crazy friend/relative/boss that you have to endure. Hopefully, one or two of these 103 ideas make it better for you.

HAPPY DOWNLOADING!

www.ingramcontent.com/pod-product-compliance
Lightning Source LLC
Chambersburg PA
CBHW061445040426
42450CB00007B/1217